My Garden

Written by David Drew
Illustrated by Chantal Stewart

Collins Educational
An imprint of HarperCollins*Publishers*

My garden needs . . .

a painter   a gardener   a vet

a gardener.

 a mechanic  a plumber  a dentist

My car needs . . .

a painter

a gardener

a vet

a mechanic.

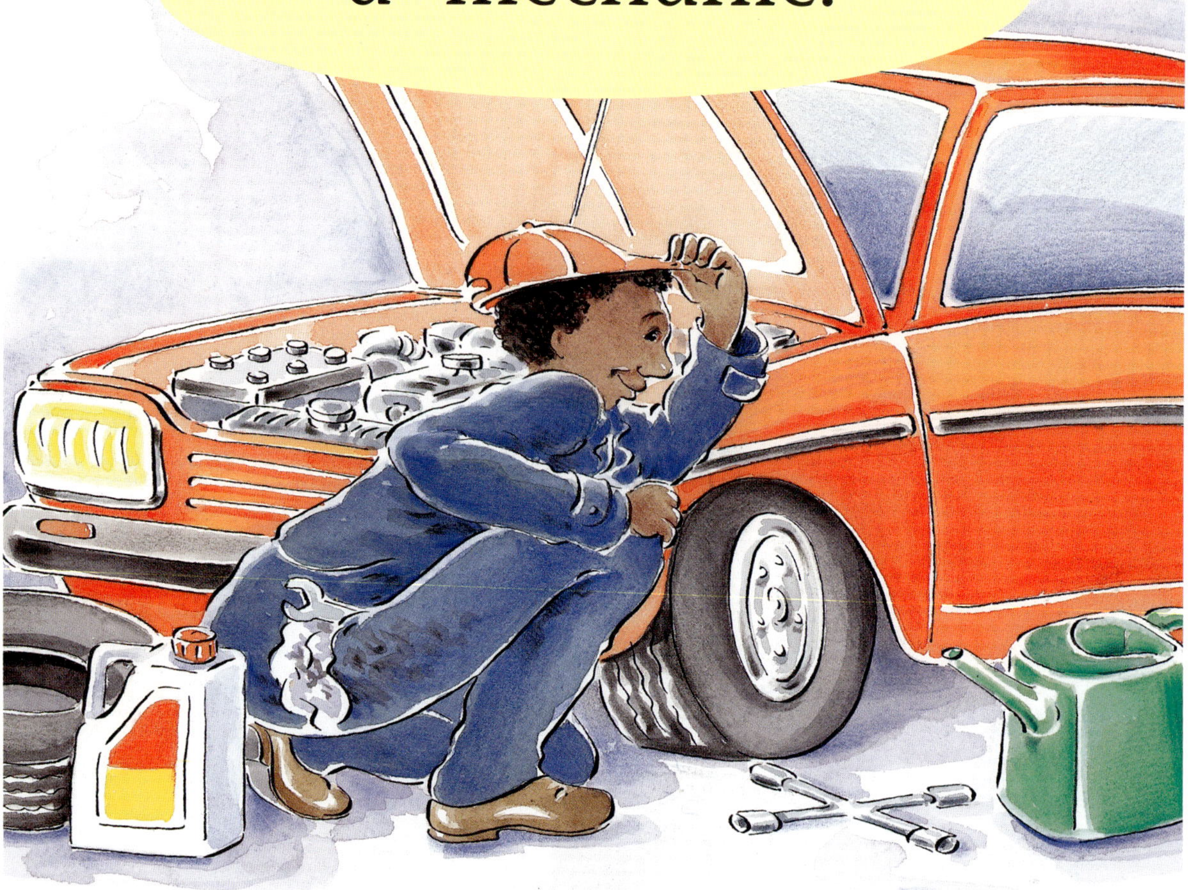

 a mechanic
 a plumber
 a dentist

"My dog needs . . ."

a painter

a gardener

a vet

a vet.

a mechanic   a plumber   a dentist

"My tap needs..."

a painter

a gardener

a vet

a plumber.

a mechanic   a plumber   a dentist

My house needs . . .

 a painter

 a gardener

 a vet

a painter.

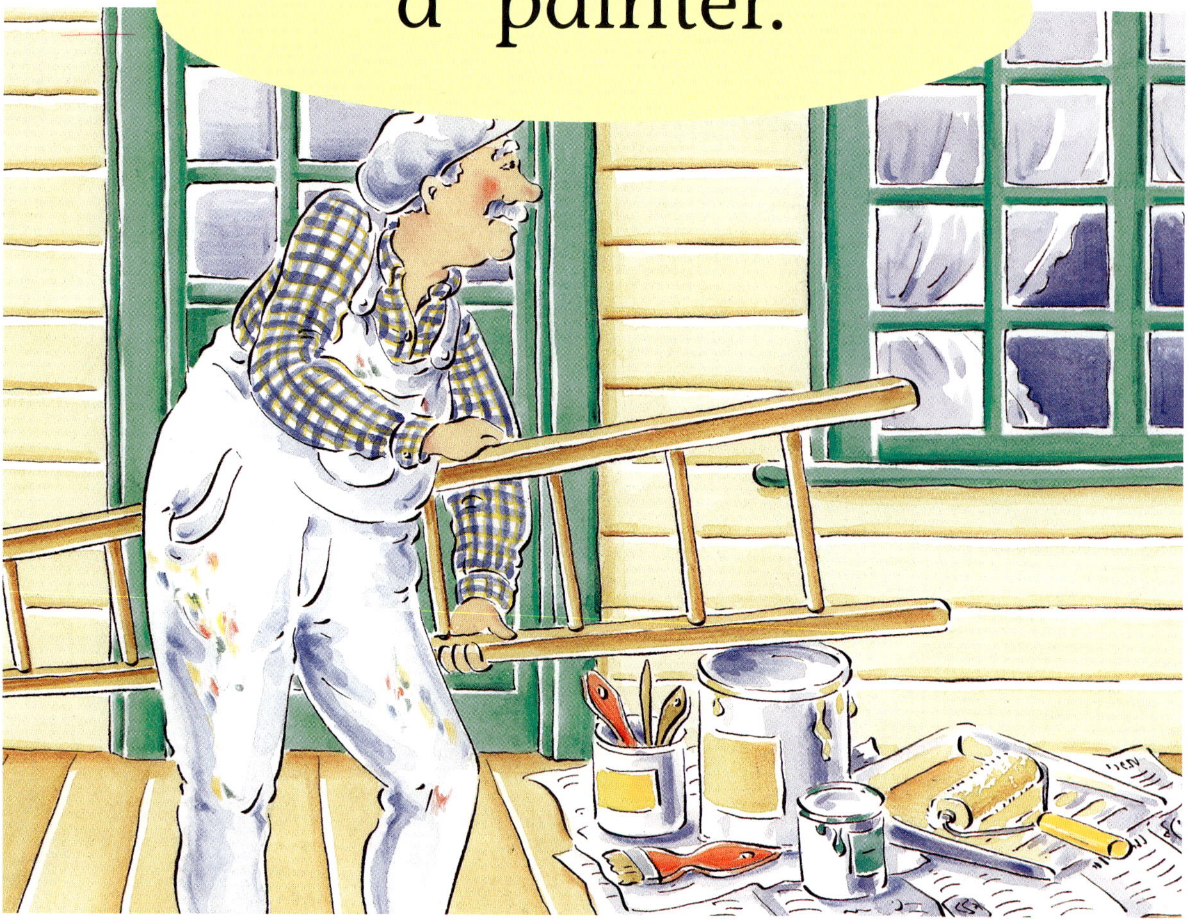

a mechanic a plumber a dentist

My tooth needs . . .

a painter   a gardener    a vet

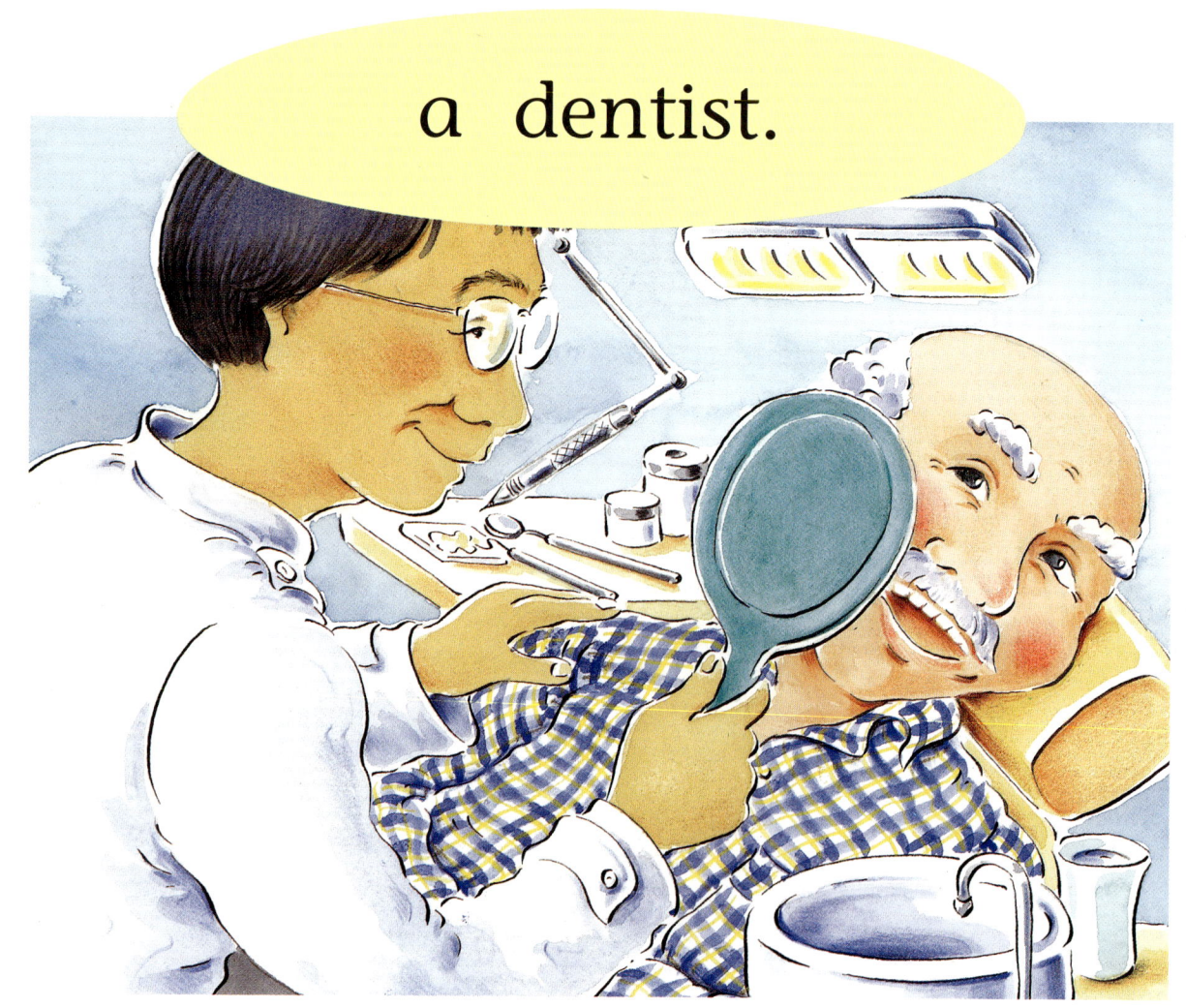

Who else do we need?

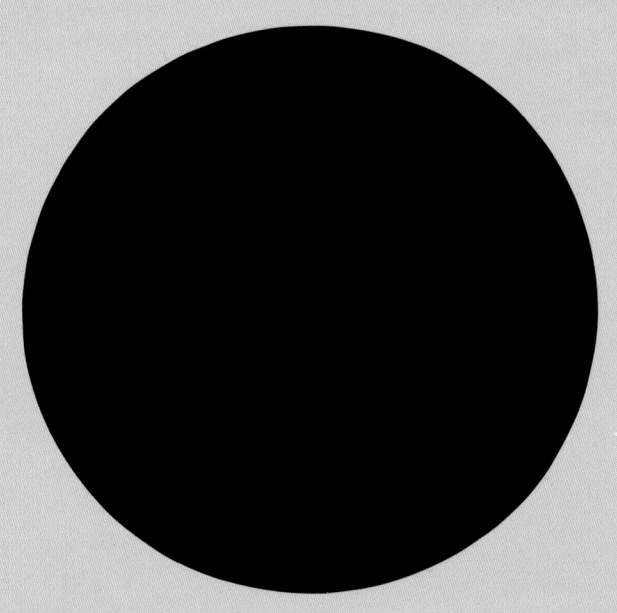

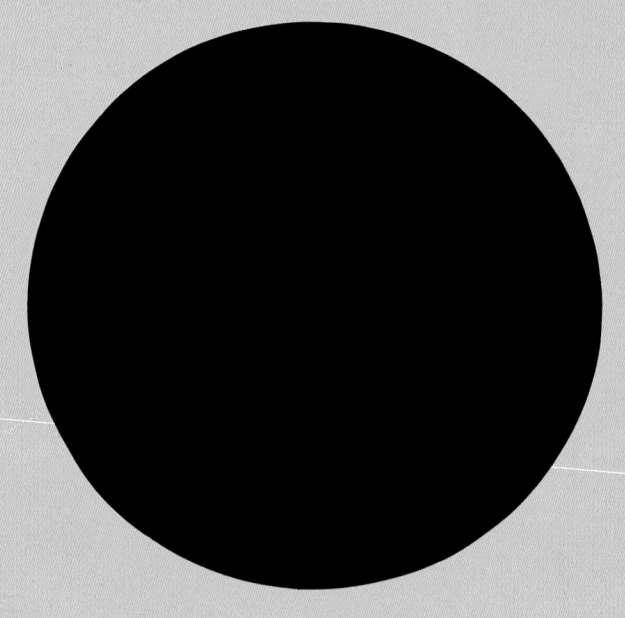

farmer

doctor baker

teacher

cleaner TV reporter